Why Do Cats Wear Pajamas?

Why Do Cats Wear Pajamas?

Written and Illustrated
by Karen Brown

**Andrews McMeel
Publishing**

Kansas City

01 02 03 04 05 TWP 10 9 8 7 6 5 4 3 2 1

ISBN: 0-7407-0760-4

Library of Congress Catalog Card Number: 00-108472

ATTENTION: SCHOOLS AND BUSINESSES

To
my slinky agent,
Betsy Amster

H<small>E</small>

was tall, exotic, and intense. He had the best body I had ever seen. He was aloof and mysterious one moment, and disarmingly natural the next. He was selfish, he was vain, and he never once put anything back where he found it.

He stayed out all night but he never lied to me. We had, as they say, *an understanding*.

But our affair was not without its obstacles.

The first, of course, was the difference in our ages. On the day we met, I had just had my ninth birthday and he was a wide-eyed seven-week-old.

And we had a bit of a problem with size, for fully grown he stood scarcely a foot high when measured from his sleek tabby shoulder. But he was so smart and funny, so affectionate and sweet, so magnificent and original, that I have secretly looked for him in the soul of every man I have met since.

This was Esmond, and he was my first cat.

Have you noticed that people generally love cats or they hate cats? Have you ever met anyone who was genuinely indifferent to them?

I haven't.

I don't think it's possible to be indifferent to an entire race of beings who are all remarkably alike and all entirely unique.

And so this is for all the Esmonds,
and the Fluffies,
and the Tigers,
and the Freds,
and the Chesters,
and the Bozos,
and the Cocos,
and the Bobs,

who are all remarkably alike and entirely unique,
all smart and funny, all magnificent
and original, and all immortal, in their little
earth-bound hearts, to those of us who have
loved them.

W_{HO}

was the fattest cat in history?

It was Himmy, a male tabby house cat
from Queensland, Australia.

Himmy weighed 46 pounds, 15¼ ounces.
He measured 33 inches
around his waist
and was 38 inches long.

Which cat had the most kittens?

Dusty, a tabby cat
from Bonham, Texas,
produced 420 kittens in her lifetime.
Dusty was born in 1935.

Which cat had the most kittens
in a single litter?

On August 7, 1970, a Burmese-Siamese mix
in Wescote, England, produced
a litter of nineteen kittens.

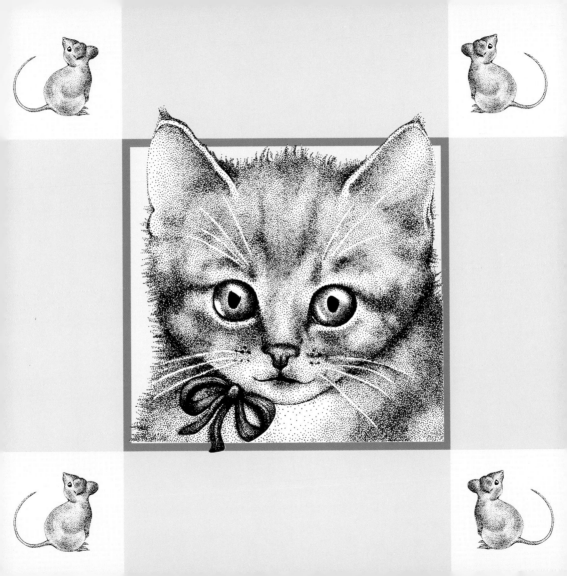

How many kittens
can the average cat have?

A female cat can have anywhere
from twelve to twenty-eight
kittens a year, or three to seven
kittens every four months.

How long do cats nurse?

Generally, healthy kittens
are fully weaned at
eight weeks.

What
is the only continent
in the world
where cats are not
indigenous?

Antarctica.

W HICH
cat caught the most mice?

A female tortoiseshell named Towser, owned by a distillery in Scotland, killed 28,899 mice in her lifetime.

D_o

cats make good vegetarians?

No. A cat's digestive track is short and designed for a carnivorous diet. For a cat to be healthy, it must have a diet rich in meat—
meat substitutes like soy and grain products just won't do.

WHERE did cats come from?

The first cats appeared on earth about thirty-five to forty million years ago. Today, there are approximately thirty-five species of cats that range in size from the tiger, who weighs more than eight hundred pounds, to the black-footed cat, who weighs less than six pounds.

It is unusual for members of different cat species to mate and produce offspring. However, sometimes in special circumstances, closely related species can breed successfully. In some zoos, for example, lions and tigers have mated. What do zoologists call their babies?
Ligers or tions.

HO
was the most
expensive cat in the world?

It was a California
spangled cat,
purchased for $24,000 in January 1987.
This very special cat
was a model in the
Neiman Marcus
Christmas catalog.

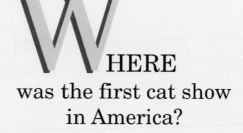

WHERE
was the first cat show
in America?

America's first cat show was held
in Madison Square Garden
in New York
in May 1895.

How many breeds of cats exist?

There are approximately one hundred recognized breeds of cats. Cat breeding is a relatively new practice, originating a little over a century ago.

Although some breeds like the Maine Coon Cat occurred "naturally" when cats were allowed to roam free and breed on their own, most breeds came about through careful selection and development. When a particularly fine or unusual kitten appeared in an otherwise normal litter, this special kitten might be bred, when grown, to create more cats with similar characteristics.

W

HY
do cats wear pajamas?

Well, they don't, of course, but cats are
the greatest sleepers
in the world of mammals.
You can almost think of their
pretty coats as a living set of very
luxurious pajamas. A healthy cat
sleeps sixteen to eighteen hours
a day, about as much as a
newborn human baby.

What
are "toms"
and "queens"?

"Toms" and "queens"
are breeders' terms
for male
and female cats.

How many toes does a cat have?

A cat has eighteen toes, five on each front
paw and four on each back paw. Cats are
one of the few animals who can extend
and retract their claws.

How high can cats jump?

An adult cat can jump about five times its
own height.

A RE

blue-eyed cats good luck?

Perhaps, but blue eyes may not be
good luck for the cat.
Blue-eyed cats, particularly cats with
white coats, are often deaf.
In some breeds, if the cat has one
blue eye and one golden eye, it will be
deaf only on the blue-eyed side.

Why do cats hate water?

In fact, not all cats
hate water and some
cats seem to enjoy
playing in it.
The Turkish Van Cat is
sometimes called the
Turkish Swimming Cat
because it seeks out
water for what appears
to be no other reason
than its enjoyment.
And the wild Bengali
Mach-Bagral, known
as the "fishing cat,"
swims and hooks fish
with its long claws.

A RE

some cats born hairless?

The only cat bred to be hairless is
the Sphynx, a breed developed from
a mutant kitten in the 1960s.
Unlike other cats, the Sphynx can perspire
through its skin and special care must be
taken by its owner to give it sponge baths
on a regular basis.
Its body temperature is also higher than
average, which is why its skin is
sometimes described as feeling like a
"suede hot water bottle."

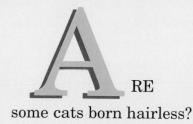

How
well
do
cats
see?

Very well, but not at first because kittens are born blind with their eyes closed. After several days, their eyes open but their vision does not develop fully for a few months. Eventually, cats develop what is known as stereoscopic vision, which allows them to judge distance with great accuracy. This special vision is part of what makes cats such great hunters.

WHY

are some gemstones
called "cat's-eyes"?

A cat's-eye is any of several
gemstones that, when cut and
polished, display a band of color
reminiscent of the eye of a cat. The
African cat's-eye, also known as
tiger's-eye, is a kind of quartz that
contains streaks of silica that look
like the pupil of a tiger's eye.

Why are cats difficult to train?

Anyone who has ever seen a cat run into the kitchen at the sound of the can opener knows that a cat can quickly learn a behavior if there is a reward involved. Cats have been trained to play the piano, walk tightropes, jump through hoops, ring bells, and perform many other very theatrical tricks.

Unlike dogs, however, cats require more than just approval if you want them to learn. Professional trainers use a variety of rewards to train cats. One of the most effective seems to be high-quality baby food, such as strained chicken.

Why do cats love catnip?

Catnip is an herb that has a powerful effect on most cats, who love to smell and roll around on the fresh plant or dried leaves. The scent seems to excite cats because it is chemically similar to the sexual pheromone secreted by female cats. The scent does not appear to affect kittens under two months old.

How

long

do

cats

live?

Cats today are living longer than ever, thanks to their caring owners. The average house cat will live between fifteen to eighteen years. The author's cat, Chester, lived to be twenty-three.

W HEN

did cats start to live with people?

The first domesticated cats were by kept by the ancient Egyptians to guard precious stores of grain from rodents. Around 1500 B.C., after a particularly large grain harvest, the reigning pharaoh needed more cats to guard his grain. It is believed that his solution was to declare all cats to be demigods. Being divine himself, only the pharaoh was allowed to own cats. Householders could enjoy their cats by day but had to take them to the grain stores to catch rodents at night, by order of the pharaoh.

What
is a
tabby
cat?

Tabby markings are distinctive stripes, swirls, and bars that appear in the patterns of many cats' coats. Tabbies are possibly the world's oldest breed and their markings are probably the most common, finding their way into purebreds and mongrels alike.

The word "tabby" is believed to be derived from "Attabiah," an area in Baghdad where a very special watered silk was made. The patterns in the silk bear some resemblance to the markings of the tabby cat.

WHY

doesn't the Manx cat have a tail?

The Manx's lack of a tail is a mutation that developed during its isolation on the Isle of Man. The gene that produced the missing tail seems to have been dominant, and as time went by tails were naturally bred out of the Manx line. The Manx developed extra long back legs, however, which help to replace the balance that a cat's tail normally helps provide.

A biblical myth says that the Manx has no tail because it was the last animal to board the Ark. An impatient Noah slammed the Ark's door on the cat's tail, chopping it off.

WHAT

were the first domesticated cats in America?

Cats were imported from Europe to the New World colonies in the 1600s in order to control the rodent population. The first domestic cats to reach the shores of America were a pair given by a French missionary to a Native American chief. The cats died without producing kittens. Breeding cats were imported from England in 1749 and their offspring became the first American house cats.

How fast
can a
cat run?

A house cat
can run in bursts
up to thirty miles
an hour.

Is

the breed called the "Ocicat" bred from real ocelots?

No. The Ocicat breed originated from the unexpected and striking result of mixing a Siamese with an Abyssinian. The breed was further developed to produce the spotted and ticked championship cats that exists today.

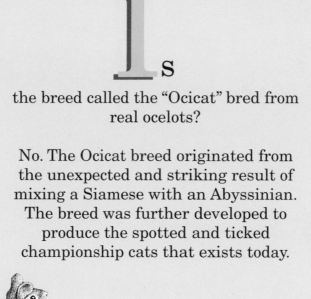

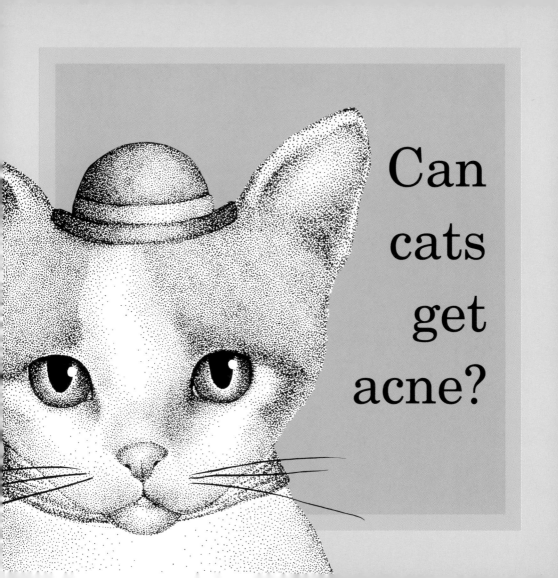

Can
cats
get
acne?

Yes. Little bumps around the cat's chin and mouth are usually caused by clinging food particles or an allergic reaction to the cat's food dish, particularly if the dish is made of plastic. This is real acne and was originally called "Aby chin" when it was diagnosed first in Abyssinians, where it was easy to see against the breed's white chin.

W ho was the most famous cat of the twentieth century?

The title probably goes to Morris, the star of the 9-Lives television commercials. He was found—sick and weak—by his trainer in an animal shelter. Morris was a natural performer and went on to win Best Animal Actor in 1973. The story of his rescue inspired the adoption of many stray and lost animals.

W hat was the longest running Broadway musical of all time?

Cats—which broke all previous performance records for a Broadway musical on June 19, 1977. It continued to play for another twenty-three years until it closed on September 10, 2000, after 7,485 performances.

Can a
cat
smell
through
its
mouth?

When a cat has a strong interest in a particular scent, it may "flehm," which means it breathes through its open mouth while wrinkling its nose. The cat may also appear unusually distracted or absorbed. Flehming seems to be a cat's reaction to sexual odors.

Flehming helps bring odors into contact with something called "Jacobson's organ," which is a little pouch located at the front of the upper palette. Humans also have a Jacobson's organ, but in humans it does not appear to have a function.

Should house cats be declawed?

No! Declawing is a surgical process that involves removing the claw and first bone of each toe. This amputation is extremely painful for the cat and can result in loss of balance, lameness, nervousness, refusal to use the litter box, and other behaviors like biting and excessive licking. It also requires that the cat be kept indoors for the rest of its life, since it cannot climb or defend itself.

As an alternative to declawing, a loving owner can trim the cat's claws. Your veterinarian can show you how to safely trim claws, which needs to be done about once a month.

Do
cats
dream?

They seem to. Anyone who has watched a cat sleep knows that cats can be quite active during sleep, twitching their ears and tails, growling, and even crying out. This activity seems to be related to REM sleep in humans, the periods during which we dream.

How much
time does
a cat spend
grooming
itself?

A healthy cat will spend almost one-third of its waking hours grooming itself.

How do cats purr?

It may seem hard to believe, but how and why cats purr is not well understood. Some researchers believe purring is caused by the action of air passing by the diaphragm muscles, the larynx, and two membrane folds behind the larynx called the false vocal cords. Others believe purring is caused by the vibrations of one or more large blood vessels in the cat's chest. The vibrations of purring occur at twenty-six cycles per second, the same as a diesel engine.

Purring is not always a sign of contentment. Cats who are ill or anxious may purr. Purring is one of the first instinctual behaviors cats demonstrate—newborn kittens purr when they nurse.

WHAT

shape is a cat's head?

Cats' heads have three basic shapes.
There are round heads, such as what we
see in Persians and many of the British
shorthairs, triangular heads like the
Siamese, and rectangular heads like the
Maine Coon Cat.

W

HAT
is a feral cat?

A feral cat is a house cat or its offspring
who have gone wild, usually
because they are lost or abandoned.

There are an estimated sixty million
feral cats in the United States.

Who

is the better hunter—a male cat or a female cat?

Females are usually the dominant hunters. Even among the big cats, the females usually make the kill, although the strongest males often eat first and longest.

Do cats always land
on their feet?

Not always, but they are particularly
good at flipping over in the air and
landing with all four feet on the ground.
Cats have elastic muscles and flexible
skeletons that absorb much of the shock
from a fall. In fact, many parts of the
cat's skeleton are held together with
muscle only, rather than with ligaments
as in humans and other animals.

What
is the
heaviest
breed of
house
cat?

The Ragdoll
is the largest,
with many
weighing over
twenty pounds.
The smallest
breed is the
Singapura,
an elegant
breed
with a silky
ticked coat,
who weighs
about six
pounds.

Are Persian cats from Persia?

An early, shorthaired ancestor of the Persian cat originated in Turkey and Iran (formerly Persia). What we consider to be the modern Persian breed developed in Europe in the 1600s as a longhaired mutation. In fact, Persians were known as "Longhairs" in the U.S. until the 1960s and still go by that name in England today.

Are cats
right-
or
left-
handed?

Cats often behave as if they were ambidextrous, although if they have a preference, it seems to be for the left paw. Some researchers believe that this makes cats right-brain dominant, which may explain some of their intuitive and dreamy qualities.

How many
teeth
does a cat have?

Thirty—
twelve incisors,
four canines, and
fourteen molars.

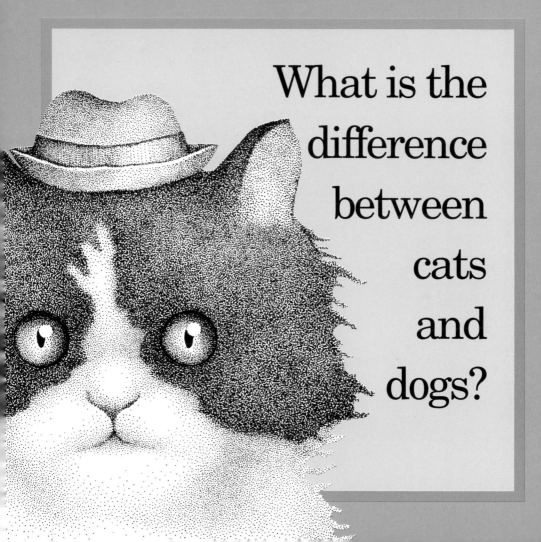

What is the difference between cats and dogs?

If you take excellent care of your dog—
if you play with him,
feed him treats,
love him and pet him—
your dog will think
you are king.

If you take excellent
care of your cat—
if you play
with him,
feed him treats,
love him
and pet him—
your cat will
think
he is king.

The author wishes to thank
her editor, Chris Schillig,
and the generous, talented staff at
Andrews McMeel for their
suggestions, enthusiasm,
and support.

Special thanks also to
Guinness World Records
for permission to use
several of the facts contained
in the book.